Truly, Madly, Deeply

Nina is terrific, successful, funny and bright. She lives in a terrible flat in North London, with bad plumbing, subsidence and a plague of rats. Her lover, Jamie, has died. Nina can't get over him. No amount of attention from new men, or a fulfilling career, or support from her friends can assuage her grief. She wants Jamie back. So he comes back, the rats move out, and that's when her problems really begin . . .

A story about loss, love, ghosts and rats, **Truly, Madly, Deeply** was written and directed by Anthony Minghella, with Juliet Stevenson as Nina and Alan Rickman as Jamie.

Anthony Minghella is the author of **A Little Like Drowning**, **Made in Bangkok**, (*Plays and Players* Best New Play 1986), **What if it's Raining?**, **The Storyteller** (Emmy and Bafta Awards 1987/88), **Hang Up** (Prix Italia 1988), and **Cigarettes and Chocolate**, (1988 Sony Award, 1988 Giles Cooper Award).

A Methuen Screenplay

First published in Great Britain as a paperback original in the
Methuen Screenplay series in 1991 by Methuen Drama, 81 Fulham
Road, London SW3 6RB and distributed in the United States of
America by HEB Inc., 361 Hanover Street, Portsmouth, New
Hampshire 03801.

ISBN 0-413-64000-0

A CIP catalogue record for this book is available
from the British Library

The front cover is from the poster for the film of **Truly, Madly, Deeply**
and shows Juliet Stevenson as Nina and Alan Rickman as Jamie, © *The
Samuel Goldwyn Company. The photographs inside the book are* © *BBC.*

'The Dead Woman' by Pablo Neruda is published in 'The Captain's
Verses' by Pablo Neruda, English translation Donald D Walsh, A
New Directions Paintbook, 1972.

Printed and bound in Great Britain
by Cox & Wyman Ltd, Cardiff Road, Reading

Anthony Minghella

Truly, Madly, Deeply

For Juliet Stevenson

Methuen Drama

Introduction

Someone once described the process of film-making to me in this way: a painter works with a paintbrush on canvas; a film-maker also has a canvas but there are eighty people hanging onto the brush. In my case I felt that the eighty people were supporting the brush, improving the strokes and generally engaged in preventing me from ruining my own picture.

No small part of the attraction of making **Truly, Madly, Deeply** was to bring together a whole family of actors and collaborators who have worked with me over the past few years. If nothing else the film is a testimony to the virtues of repeated working relationships and professional friendships. As I write this I remember that trains are another favoured metaphor in film-making. A director is like a kid with a train set. Not so. The unnerving sensation I had while making the film was of playing guard on a runaway train; a terror leavened by the knowledge that there was always fun and wisdom to be had in the dining-car. The image of a child up in the attic controlling a perfect, miniature and pretend universe is far more akin to the experience of writing.

As a child I lived with my parents above a small seaside cafe on the Isle of Wight and many of my crucial early life-experiences were played out in the public arena of the big kitchen which doubled up as sitting-room and catering thoroughfare. There were swing doors into the restaurant and every family conversation, confrontation or confession, every success, every tragedy was punctuated by an arrival or departure, a new customer emergency, full plates, dirty dishes and the gossip of the day. I played, worked, laughed, ate and cried in that arena – multicultural, classless and crazy. I remember being desperate to escape from it and there can be little accident that I fetched up in a career which enforces long stretches of privacy and quiet. Nevertheless, somewhere in the middle of making **Truly, Madly, Deeply**, on a particularly frantic and chaotic day, trying to focus on a tiny, intimate moment while interrupted by a thousand other urgencies, I realised that I had, in some way, come home; what's more, I felt peculiarly exhilarated.

I am disappointed that space prevents me from listing the entire cast and crew of the film in this publication. Many of the names have appeared in previous acknowledgements, Mark Shivas, Michael Maloney, Barrington Pheloung are longtime accomplices and, once again, Robert Cooper has tirelessly navigated a project of mine from start to finish. Alan Rickman's determination on both sides of the

camera to make the film a better one was invaluable as was John
Stothart's generous skill in the cutting room. And if I single out
Remi Adefarasin and Peter Markham from a marvellous company it
is only because their help and talent and contribution was of the
variety invisible to an audience but essential to a novice director. To
them, to the BBC, Jayne Spooner, Eleanor Drew and my agents,
Michael Peretzian in America and Louise Cooper in London, as well
as the members and staff of the remarkable Reach Group in
Swindon, special thanks.

I wrote **Truly, Madly, Deeply** for Juliet Stevenson; the film is
suffused with her spirit, her concerns and her great heart. And, as
with so much of my work over the last decade, it has been an
adventure shared and illuminated by her.

Anthony Minghella, 1991

Truly, Madly, Deeply opened in the USA and the UK in 1991, with the following cast, in order of appearance:

Nina	Juliet Stevenson
Burge	Jenny Howe
Translator	Carolyn Choa
Sandy	Bill Paterson
Titus	Christopher Różycki
Plumber	Keith Bartlett
George	David Ryall
Maura	Stella Maris
Harry	Ian Hawkes
Claire	Deborah Findlay
Jamie	Alan Rickman
Frenchman	Vania Vilers
Roberto	Arturo Venegas
Symonds	Richard Syms
Mark	Michael Maloney
Isaac	Mark Long
Freddie	Teddy Kempner
Pierre	Graeme Du-Fresne
Bruno	Frank Baker
Anthony	Tony Bluto
As themselves	Members of the Reach Group, Swindon
Midwife	Heather Williams
Maura's Baby	Henry James
Designer	Barbara Gosnold
Editor	John Stothart
Original music	Barrington Pheloung
Featured music	J S Bach
Director of Photography	Remi Adefarasin
Executive Producer	Mark Shivas
Producer	Robert Cooper
Director	Anthony Minghella

A BBC Films Production presented by The Samuel Goldwyn Company.

Ext: London underground. Night.

Nina *emerges from a tube station and sets off into the night.*

Ext: London streets and **Nina***'s flat. Night.*

Nina *is walking quickly down some alleyway steps. It's night.*

Nina *feels threatened by stray noises, footsteps, the dark. She crosses the Archway Bridge. She walks down a street.*

Nina (*VO*) Mostly when I'm walking, at night, or anyway, alone, if I'm frightened, then he'll turn up, he'll, he'll talk, about what I'm doing, you know, some advice, he'll say – 'Don't be frightened. I've told you – walk in the middle of the road at night'.

She goes into the middle of the road.

And I will, I move over to the middle of the road, or, I don't know, he'll say – 'It's a disgrace, this street is a disgrace, there's no proper lighting, have you written, you must write!' He's always forthright, I mean he always was forthright so I suppose that's not, but, you know, he'll also speak in Spanish to me, which is odd because he couldn't speak Spanish – and I would have been feeling low, you know, very alone and hopeless and – and then he's there, his presence, and it's okay, it's fine, and I don't mind and he tells me he loves me.

She's at the front gate of the building which contains her flat. She opens the gate and goes inside.

And then he's not there anymore.

Burge (*VO*) And then how do you feel?

Nina (*VO*) Okay, fine, well, I feel looked after, I suppose, watched over. You see, he never says anything profound or earth-shattering, you know, he doesn't say *well God thinks this* or –

Int: Therapist's room. Day.

Grey sky outside the window. Camera pushes down to **Nina** *who is sitting on a heavy armchair, next to a Georgian picture window.*

Her therapist **Burge** *presides.*

Nina – or about the planet or world events or, or *there's no God*, or, it's all *go to bed, brush your teeth*, or the way I'm brushing my teeth, because I always brush them side to side and I'll be doing that and he'll say *down at the top, come on, down at the top, up from the bottom* or, lock the back door, *cierra la puerta de atrás.*

Burge What's that?

Nina Lock the back door.

Burge Is it significant, do you think, he says that in Spanish?

Nina No.

Int: **Nina**'s *flat. Bathroom. Night.*

Nina *finishes brushing her teeth. She rinses the brush and returns it to the glass.*

Jamie (*OOV*) *Cierra la puerta de atrás.*

Nina (*smiles*) I did. It's locked.

Burge (*VO*) How long ago did Jamie die?

Nina *wipes her mouth with a flannel.*

Burge (*VO*) Nina?

Nina *pulls the cord and plunges the room into black.*

And on the black screen we get –

Burge (*VO over credits*) Jamie, when was it he died?

Music is playing. Bach's Sonata No 3 for Cello (Viol de gamba) and Piano, 2nd Movement.

The cello is supple, straining with emotion.

We're still on black, but the camera is moving and finds, in black and white, a cello in close, hands coaxing the strings. It's **Jamie**.

He plays and we see him full length, bent over his instrument intent. Pull out and then freeze the image.

Int: **Nina**'s *living room. Morning.*

Keep pulling out and find that the image is now a photograph inside a frame and that the photograph is in **Nina**'s *bedroom.*

As the image freezes to become this photograph, the cello line is replaced by a voice, humming.

The camera tracks across the bedroom, across the hall, past the bathroom and kitchen to discover **Nina** *playing the piano.*

By the piano, a cello leans against the wall. She half sings the cello part. This is clearly something of a ritual for her.

The flat is tasteful, not without humour, untidy, evidence of a chaotic life. The Latin American countries make a significant cultural contribution.

There is a work area, a table loaded with files and papers, a pinboard with some industrial instruction sheets, a couple of record sleeves.

Nina *closes her eyes as she vocalises the cello part. Something makes her open them. She stops playing, freezes. Her eyes go glassy.*

A RAT scampers across the top of the piano. Obviously a Bach fan.

Nina *regards it calmly for a second or two. Then she gasps and stares at the rat. She stops playing the piano.*

Int: Translation agency. Day.

A kind of neighbourhood translation supermarket, where you can get walk-in advice and translations in twenty-eight languages in a small scruffy open-plan office. It's the end of the day and the office is closing.

Sandy *is boss.*

Nina *works at a computer on her desk. The* **Translator** *prepares to go.*

Translator N'night, bye.

Nina Are you off, Carolyn? 'Bye.

Translator Yeah. See you tomorrow.

Nina N'night.

Translator Night, Sandy.

Sandy Oh, 'bye Carolyn. 'Bye.

Nina *goes back to the screen.* **Sandy** *is ready to go. He comes over. He is a lovable, maudlin Scot whose life is a disaster.*

Sandy I like your hair.

Nina What?

Sandy Your hair, it looks, is it different? Or is it the earrings? They're terrific. They look, sort of, are they sort of Inca?

Nina Sandy – what are you talking about?

Sandy Are you depressed?

Nina No.

Sandy I don't just love you because you translate my postcards, you know.

Nina I know.

Sandy You see everybody's just a wee bit concerned about you.

Nina Everybody who?

Sandy 'Cause you've disappeared. You've gone to ground. You don't come out to play anymore. You don't invite people round, you look terrible.

Nina Except for my hair.

Sandy Actually, Nina, your hair – well, your hair was never your strong point. Is it still Jamie?

Nina (*thrown*) What?

Sandy I can understand that. Lord knows I miss Gabriella and I hated her and I still miss her but you know I can understand that. You know – you've got to get out – unless you get out, you'll never meet anybody.

Nina Okay. Okay, darling. Thanks. Thanks.

They hug.

Sandy So, come on, come on, have a wee drink with your Uncle Sandy.

Nina *goes to the door.*

Nina (*distressed*) Sandy, I can't. I can't. I just can't.

Int: **Nina**'s *flat. Hall and living room. Night.*

Nina *goes to the elaborate collection of locks and bolts at her front door.* **Titus**, *her carpenter friend, is outside.*

Nina (*opening the door*) Hi. (*At the lateness of the visit.*) Everything okay?

Titus *is Polish and earnest. He examines the locks and bolts.*

Titus Good. Very safe now.

Nina Oh, yes – I'm really much happier with the door.

Titus Take ten men to break down this door.

Nina Titus, it's nearly midnight.

Titus Yes, I come to see if you still want me in the morning.

Nina Oh yes, I do, actually please. Yeah, I can't close any of my kitchen cabin – oh and, Titus listen I've got rats, I've either got two massive rats who never stop eating, or about two thousand with normal, who are on a calorie controlled diet.

She wanders through into the living room, from which it's possible to see the kitchen area.

Nina I had this man come this morning and he put down poison, he said it was enough to knock out half of North London, and it's disappearing. Look.

She picks up one of the foil containers and shows it to him.

Titus I'm missing Poland.

Nina Right.

Titus Sometimes I think I hate Poland, but then a song goes through my head, some music, or the taste, I remember taste of Polish bread of (*Shrugs.*) a man should never drink. He remembers only his country, his mother, his lovers.

Nina Yeah. I'm going to bed. I'm bushed. I've had a – it's been a really busy day.

Titus You are the only beautiful woman I meet in London.

Nina Absolutely right. That's got nothing to do with the drink. I am the only beautiful woman in London. Ni-night. See you in the morning.

Titus In my country when we want to be rid of rats we do not use poison – we dance. To drive the rats away we – we dance.

And **Titus** *begins to dance, heavy, drunk, splendid, romantic. Involves many solemn claps. The music is 'Bleeding Heart' – traditional.*

Nina *sinks onto the floor. But she enjoys the performance.* **Titus** *takes his coat.*

Titus I would be surprised if the rats will come back.

Int: **Nina**'s *bedroom. Night.*

Nina *is in bed. A rat toddles up the bed along the duvet, perilously close to* **Nina**'s *head.*

Nina *is disturbed by the sound. Her eyes flash wide. In the darkness.*

Nina (*quietly*) Oh my *God.*

Int: **Nina**'s *living room. Morning.*

Nina *is wrapped in the duvet in the living room. She slept on the sofa. She embraces a cricket bat. She's fast asleep. She's had a difficult night.*

Int: **Nina**'s *bathroom. Morning.*

Nina *looks at the tray of rat poison. She examines herself in the mirror. Is not impressed.*

She bends over the bath, puts the mat on the floor, and opens the hot tap. Nothing happens. She tries the cold tap. Steaming brown water trickles through, accompanied by a loud knocking sound.

Ext: **Nina**'s *street and flat. Morning.*

Sandy *cycles along the street up to* **Nina**'s *building. He dismounts and props his bicycle up inside the gate.*

He stumbles up the front steps.

Int: **Nina**'s *hall. Morning.*

All the floorboards in the hall are up. The front door is open.

A **Plumber** *is under the floorboards.*

Sandy *comes through the door. He's carrying some files and material for translation.*

He steps apologetically over the **Plumber**.

Sandy Sorry. Sorry. Is Nina around?

Plumber Through there.

Sandy Thanks.

Int: **Nina***'s living room. Morning.*

Nina, *dressed, is at the table eating borshch.*

Titus *has practically dismantled the kitchen and is working away, hammer, saw and sawdust.*

Sandy *is confused.*

Sandy Nina?

Nina (*pleased*) Sandy.

Sandy What's going on?

Nina Well, the fridge is still working. That's what I keep telling myself. The fish fingers are frozen.

Sandy (*sympathetically*) Oh, Nina, this flat, it's not been very, really, has it? Who's the chappie in the joists?

Nina He's the plumber, little problem with the water. Apart from anything else it's gone brown. Titus is trying to make the kitchen doors fit the cabinets, you've met Titus? – Titus, this is Sandy – Sandy runs the agency.

Titus *nods.*

Sandy Hello, Titus.

Titus Hello.

Sandy Good work.

Nina And George is here somewhere. George? No, the whole place is falling to bits. It's a disaster. Why did I buy it, Sandy? You told me, Jamie told me, everybody told me.

George *appearing, holding the foil trays.*

George Nina, this is very important. (*Sees* **Sandy**.) Hello.

Nina George, this is Sandy. He's my boss.

Sandy Hello, George.

George Have you touched these containers?

Nina No.

George You haven't emptied them out or . . . ?

Nina No.

George (*in a continuous breath*) We've got a very serious problem here,

Nina, we're talking a lot of rodents, we're talking infestation, we may even be talking nesting. Could I make a telephone call?

Nina Sure.

Sandy What's this, mice?

Nina No, no. (*She indicates the size of these creatures.*)

Sandy Rats?! Oh, my God.

Nina I have to move out.

Titus Sandy, you want Borshch?

Nina Have some. Titus says it's the answer to all our problems.

Sandy (*accepting the Borshch*) Borshch? Thanks. Nina, I've had a little postcard from Charlie. Can you spare a few minutes?

Nina Sandy, you've got to learn Spanish.

Sandy I know.

Nina It's so perverse to run a language agency, speak, how many languages do you speak? but not – I mean it's your son, you've got to understand what he's telling you . . .

Sandy I know.

Nina I mean, in the end, that was the problem with you and Gabriella, you couldn't say anything to each other.

Sandy (*solemn*) No, no, that was its strength. It was when we started to communicate it went wrong. Before that it was terrific. Sign language. It was great. Voilà.

Nina You're a twerp.

There's a whole pile of stuff besides the postcard.

Nina What's all this?

Sandy *prodding it perfunctorily.*

Sandy Work, it's urgent, it's stuff, it's urgent so I brought it with me, it's some manuals and, whatever, but the postcard, can you just sight read the postcard, Nina, because I'm beginning to have an anxiety attack.

Nina (*reading*) 'Dear Daddy . . .'

Sandy Where does it say that?

Nina *Querido papá*. There.

Sandy Fantastic.

Nina 'Dear Daddy, we are spending our holiday in Mar del Plata' . . . lovely, supposed to be beautiful . . . 'I am swimming in the sea and do not, I'm not wearing . . .' uh, what's the name of those, 'I'm not wearing . . .'

Sandy Trunks?

Nina Things, floats. 'Mario is teaching me to swim underwater.'

Sandy Bastard.

Nina 'We're staying in a big hotel which has a television in the bathroom.'

Sandy Oh – that's the thing with Gabriella, give her a television in the bathroom, doesn't that make you laugh, doesn't that make you spew after all that stuff about materialism, a television in the bathroom!

Nina (*ploughing on*) 'Last night we went to see a football match and had a barbecue which gave me diarrhoea.'

Sandy That is terrible. Because Mario, who's a bastard, that's beyond dispute, he's absolutely and manifestly a bastard, is in loco parentis, is he not? Instead he's poisoning my son.

Nina 'I'm having a great time. Wish you were here. Lots of love, Charlie.'

Sandy *after a pause, bleak.*

Sandy Yeah. Yeah. Yeah.

Nina (*nicely*) He's having a great time.

Sandy I have to write back. Nina, would you help me write back?

Nina (*exasperated*) If you promise me you'll make an effort to learn Spanish.

Sandy Si, si. Thank you. You're a good person.

Sandy *hugs* **Nina**.

Titus *leans over the kitchen balcony, wielding a hammer.*

Titus How is soup? Fantastic?

Nina It's fantastic.

Sandy Fantastic.

Titus *ladling some more food onto their plates.*

Titus I tell her last night Nina she is beautiful woman.

Sandy She is beautiful. You are.

Nina (*embarrassed*) Okay.

George *reappears.*

George I think she's beautiful.

Plumber Who's this who's beautiful?

George We're talking about Nina.

Plumber Yeah, she is.

Nina (*embarrassed*) Guys. What is this.

Ext: Walled garden. Morning.

Nina *is taking her laundry into the tiny garden area.*

Int: Kitchen area. Morning.

The four men, **Titus**, **Sandy**, **George** *and the* **Plumber** *are doing the washing up.*

They survey **Nina** *benevolently as she pegs out her washing.*

Sandy (*washing*) She really loved him, tragic. And, you know, he was young, he was younger than me, so, it was really cruel, harsh. One minute he had a sore throat, next minute he's having an examination, next minute he's stopped breathing. The anaesthetist couldn't get the tube down. If he'd had a wee suck at a Strepsil it would never have happened.

Titus (*drying*) I think she loves me. I think now she does not know yet, but . . .

Titus *makes a gesture of blossoming.*

Plumber (*also drying*) Do you like washing?

Sandy Yes. I love getting my hands in warm water.

Plumber I like drying.

Titus Also me.

George Me too.

Sandy Look at this water. It's brown.

Plumber It's a miracle there's any water.

Sandy This is a terrible flat.

Ext: **Nina**'s *walled garden. Morning.*

Outside **Nina** *pegs up her clothes. As she pegs her wet shirt to the line it obliterates her vision.*

The breeze fills the shirt, puffing out the arms.

Nina (*VO*) . . . or I find that I've just been sitting with my head in my hands and an hour has gone by, or longer, like this (*Demonstrating.*) – with the heel of my palm pressed into my eyes and I'm completely numb –

Int: **Burge**, *the therapist. Morning.*

Nina *sits in the chair by a window. The sky outside is visible.*

Nina – and the kettle can be boiling away, or the telephone, um – and I'm crying, I'm crying. I mean I can be on the tube and somebody says what's the matter? and there are tears, it's ridiculous. I miss him. I just miss him. I miss him. I miss him. I know I shouldn't do this.

She's weeping. It starts as tears dissociated from her tone of voice and gradually takes over, making it impossible for her to continue.

Nina I'm in the sitting room and I think there's no point going to bed, he's not there, or I'm in bed, I think there's no point getting up, it's anger, isn't it, it's rage, it's rage. I get so angry with people, other people, other people in love, or out of love, or wasting love, and women with children, growing children, fertile, but most of all I'm angry with him. I'm so angry with him. I can't forgive him for not being here. I can't – (*And she can't continue.*) Oh God.

Burge *lets her weep.* **Nina** *weeps and weeps. It goes on and on.*

Burge *sits in silence.* **Burge** *switches off the tape recorder. Says nothing.*

Nina, *snapping out of her mood.*

Nina Oh God. I've run over, haven't I? I'm sorry. Sorry. I'm fine, actually. I am fine. Oh God, I'm late. Listen, I'll see you next Tuesday. Thanks.

Takes a tissue from **Burge**'s *box, checking for permission.*

Nina Can I?

She blows her nose and starts to go.

Nina Bye.

Ext: Park. Morning.

Nina *walks with* **Maura**. *English lessons.*

Maura We walk.

Nina We do walk. Yeah.

Maura We looking at things.

Nina (*correcting*) *Are* looking.

Maura Yes.

Nina Say it. (*For* **Maura** *to repeat.*) We are looking at things.

Maura We are looking at things.

Nina So, what things can we see?

Maura Ah, we can see – trees.

Nina Good, we can see trees.

Maura Yeah, uh, people.

Nina Good. We can see some people.

Maura And, we can see some people. Can see cielo – ah cielo. Uh, no me lo digas.

Nina Ss – sky.

Maura Sky, sky.

Nina Very good.

Maura We can see the sky and the . . . nubes – i nubes!

Nina (*translating*) Clouds.

Maura (*trying*) Clowed.

Nina (*carefully*) Clouds.

Maura (*better*) Cloudds, yeah.

Nina Yeh. (*Looking.*) Yeah, that's right, Maura, we can see the clouds in the sky.

They look up at the sky. Exquisite, delicate clouds.

Int: **Nina***'s kitchen/living room. Day.*

Nina *is in the kitchen. Her nephew,* **Harry***, eleven, sits on the fridge.*

Nina *puts her fingers to her lips, opens a Mars bar, stuffs it in* **Harry***'s mouth. He grins.*

The sound of the vacuum cleaner distracts **Nina***. It's* **Claire***, her sister and friend.*

Nina What are you doing?

Nina *goes down into the living room.*

Claire It's no problem. We can gossip while we're cleaning.

Nina Claire, I've had plumbers – who're coming back, carpenters, rat catchers and apparently now there's subsidence in one of the supporting walls . . . being house proud gets a touch difficult.

Claire Well, vacuuming won't hurt. Leave me alone. I like cleaning.

Nina You're just like Ma.

Claire I am not. Shut up. You've always liked messing, I've always liked cleaning. I wish you'd let me help you more, I could always pop round and –

Nina *goes back to the kitchen.*

Nina No thanks.

Claire Harry, what're you doing?

Harry *is putting his hand into a tray of rat poison.*

Nina (*dashing across*) That's rat poison! Harry! Harry, that's poison!

Claire *dashing across, the unattended Hoover, going berserk.*

Claire God!

Harry, *looking a little sheepish.*

Claire Did you eat any of this stuff, oh God, did you?

Harry *shakes his head.*

Claire What's that in your mouth? Spit it out! Spit it out!

Claire *rinses* **Harry**'s *mouth.*

Nina That's chocolate, the poison's purple. (*Stabs at her own chest.*) My fault.

Claire (*admonishing*) Sit down. Just sit down for God's sake, and try not to – He's impossible!

Nina *leans over the balcony and kisses* **Harry**'s *head.*

Nina But you love him.

Claire I love him, but he's impossible. I don't always love him. Just try not to poison yourself for five minutes.

They all sit down, after **Claire** *has wrestled with the Hoover.*

Oh Nina, how can you have rats?

Nina It's a personality defect.

Claire I'm serious.

Nina I haven't spoken to them, Claire. I tried, but they won't answer. 'What are you doing here?' Nothing. It's the poison. They're sulking.

Claire There's an odour. I have to say. There's a strong odour. Even Harry noticed.

Nina (*exasperated*) Well the rats are dying, Claire. That's basically the problem on the smell front.

Claire I wish you'd come and stay with us. You could have people in and have it all done properly, or sell it. I can't bear to think of you living here all on your own.

Nina I'm fine.

Claire It's not as if Jamie ever lived here.

Nina It's got nothing to do with Jamie. Honestly, darling. Thank you, but I'm fine. You know if I came and lived with you, we'd drive each other bonkers, I mean, anyway where would I actually stay?

Claire It is a small house. It's the kids. I say all that but I, sometimes I wish I could escape somewhere myself. No, you're right, it's a stupid idea. I'll come and live here, and the men can all . . . what do you think?

Nina How's Nick?

Claire Yes. He's busy. Do you know about Everest?

Harry Dad's going to climb Mount Everest.

Nina You're joking . . . when?

Claire Well, after Christmas sometime.

Nina When's the baby due?

Claire (*defensive*) Oh no, no, the baby'll be two or three months by then. It's fine. It's fine. He probably won't go. He's hopeless with babies anyway, so I –

Nina I can't sell the flat. Nobody's buying even nice flats. Only a lunatic would, anyway I like it. I like it.

Nina *comes to sit on the sofa beside* **Claire**.

Harry *has come over and arranged himself on* **Nina**'s *lap*.

Harry (*nicely*) I like it.

Nina Exactly. Harry likes it.

Harry It's big.

Nina Oh – so are you. (*To* **Harry**.) What's the verdict on a new baby?

Harry I don't mind.

Nina You're looking fab. How's school?

Claire He's worried because he doesn't think there'll be room in our bed for four.

Nina (*squeezing him*) Course there is. Shove, that's the secret. Tactical use of the elbow.

Claire He's doing brilliantly at school. He loves it.

Nina (*frowning*) You're not getting posh.

Harry No.

Nina Good. Say bum and Trotsky twice a day before meals.

Claire Harry, don't. Have you told Nina about your lessons? He's having cello lessons.

Nina (*suddenly tight*) Oh, really?

Claire Isn't that great? (*To* **Harry**) Are you going to ask Nina?

Harry (*shy*) You ask her.

Nina What's this?

Claire Well, Harry was wondering, he's having these lessons and, at some point – well, the school provides boys with an instrument – until you sort of decide whether or not it's serious, whether or not the boy is going to persevere . . . but then, obviously he'll need his own cello.

Nina Yeah – so what are you getting at?

Claire Well, obviously say if this is a bad idea, but we did wonder, we were wondering whether Jamie's cello, is that a terrible idea? You don't play it and perhaps . . .

Nina *in an almost unrecognisable tone.*

Nina You want me to give you Jamie's cello?

Claire No, not give, no. No. Um. I mean either for Harry to borrow it or we'll try and buy it or –

Nina Have you any idea how much that cello is worth?

Claire Well I know it's a good one, of course –

Nina (*distraught*) I can't believe you'd be so insensitive. That's practically all I've got of him. It is him. It is him. It's like asking me to give you his body.

Claire (*over this*) – Oh Nina, it isn't –

Nina (*ploughing on*) Well, anyway, you can't have it.

Claire Okay. I'm sorry. I'm sorry. You're right it was . . .

Nina (*losing her grip*) You should never have asked. It's so horrible.

Claire I had no idea you'd react so . . . Nina . . . Nina . . .

Nina *is closing right down. Paralysed.*

Int: **Nina**'s *living room. Night.*

Nina *sits on the floor, holding the cello in her arms. She puts it on the floor, and goes to the piano. She plays the Bach duet.*

The cello part comes in, sweet, intense, moving.

Nina *comes to terms with the fact that there does really seem to be a cello playing in the room. She does not, dare not, turn round.*

But then the cello stops. Her face falls. She lets out a sharp sigh and stops playing herself. She leans forward and puts her head in her hands.

Jamie *is there, tangible, loving her, pulling her up, embracing her, and she cries and laughs and cries and can't believe what's happening.*

Int: **Nina**'s *kitchen. Night.*

Jamie *and* **Nina** *sit on the kitchen floor, cuddled up together.*

Jamie I kept thinking – just my luck – die of a sore throat.

Nina But dying, actually dying – what's it like?

Jamie Dying's okay. It was the general anaesthetic I didn't like.

Nina I'm serious.

Jamie So am I. I don't know, maybe I didn't die properly, maybe that's why I can come back . . . It was like walking behind a glass wall while everybody else got on with missing me. It didn't hurt. You know I'm very sensitive to pain.

Nina Um.

Jamie It really didn't hurt.

Nina But where do you go? I mean, do you go to Heaven, or what?

Jamie I don't think so.

Nina I can't take all this in. Where do I start? Are you here? You are here?

Jamie I am here.

Nina Are you staying?

Jamie Well, I think so. I'd like to. Is that all right?

Nina It's fantastic. Can I kiss you?

Jamie Yeah.

They kiss.

Nina Your lips are a bit cold.

Jamie Actually, I'm fantastically cold. That's one thing I've really noticed. This flat is freezing.

Nina Well, the heating's on. It's supposed to be on, anyway.

Jamie I've gotta tell you – this is a terrible flat.

Nina I know.

Jamie It's terrible. Honestly, Nina, you're hopeless. And something else is really bothering me too. You've got red bills. Red gas, red phone . . . it's not clever.

Nina I know. I know.

Jamie And you never lock the back door. It's driving me crazy.

Nina I'm going. I'm going.

And she does, unravelling herself from him.

Ext: **Nina***'s walled garden. Night.*

Nina *is fiddling outside, bringing in washing.*

Jamie *appears in the doorway. Watches her.*

Jamie (*soft now*) Thank you for missing me.

Nina I have. I do. I did.

Jamie I know. But the pain, your pain, I couldn't bear that. There's a little girl, I see this little girl from time to time, Alice, who's three, three and a half, and she's great, everybody loves her, makes a big fuss, but she's not spoiled, well she wasn't spoiled, and she was knocked over, and her parents, and her family, the friends from kindergarten – she used to go to this park – and she was telling me, she, they made an area in the park, gave the money for swings and little wooden animals, and there are these plaques on each of the, on the sides of the swing, the bottom of the horse. 'From Alice's Mum and Dad. In loving memory of Alice who used to play here.' And, of course, Alice goes back there all the time. You see parents take their child off the swing and see the sign and then they hold on to their son and daughter so tightly, clinging on for dear life, and yet the capacity to love, people have, what happens to it?

Nina I don't know.

Jamie (*wry*) I blame the government.

Nina What?

Jamie The government.

Nina What's the government got to do with anything?

Jamie I hate the bastards.

Nina (*incredulous*) You've died and you're still into party politics?

Jamie (*proudly*) I still attend meetings.

Nina Oh God.

Jamie (*pointedly*) Which is more than can be said for some other people.

The doorbell rings.

Nina That's my doorbell.

Jamie It's a bit late. You expecting somebody?

Nina Uh no.

Jamie Oh – I'll make myself scarce.

Int: **Nina**'s *front door. Night.*

Nina *opens the door to discover* **Titus**.

Titus I make decision. We go to Paris. Make love for one week.

Nina Titus.

She starts to laugh. It's not cruel. It's a nice, helpless laugh. She's very touched.

Nina You're fab. You're so sweet.

Titus *smiles, hands her a plane ticket.*

Nina Oh Titus, I can't go to Paris with you. (*At the ticket.*) Oh dear.

Titus Why? You – you don't like Paris? You don't want to make love?

Nina (*teasing*) For a week? (*Then gently.*) No, no, no, no, I love Paris. No, it's got nothing to do with your offer which is very kind, no, which is more than kind, it's lovely. It's just that I'm not really looking for a lover, to be . . . It's not you. I'd say the same to anybody.

Titus Can I come in?

Nina No.

Titus Just for talk.

Nina No, really. It's too late.

Titus Now I am depressed.

Nina I'm sorry.

Titus I bought tickets. I am man with big emotion, big heart.

Nina I know, Titus. Thank you.

Titus (*resigned now*) Well. I love you. You follow.

Nina I follow.

Nina *closes the door.*

Int: **Nina***'s flat. Hall to living room. Night.*

Nina *comes down the hall.* **Jamie** *appears to have disappeared. She explores the living room and kitchen.*

Nina Jamie?

She looks more carefully.

Nina Jamie?

She's suddenly desperate.

Nina Jamie, please, where are you?

Int: Landing outside **Nina***'s flat. Night.*

From where he crouches, outside **Nina***'s door,* **Titus** *hears this plaintive call.*

Nina (*OOV*) Jamie? Please, come back.

Titus *listens, frowns.*

Int: **Nina***'s bedroom. Night.*

Nina *sits on her bed, her hand over her eyes.*

Jamie (*casually*) Who was that?

And he's sitting beside her on the bed. **Nina** *screams.*

Nina (*exasperated*) Is this going to be your party trick?

Jamie Sounded like a man's voice.

Nina Titus. It was Titus. Don't worry. (*As an afterthought.*) He's Polish.

Jamie Bit late to come round.

Nina That's what I told him.

Jamie So, what – is he in love with you?

Nina I don't think so, no.

Jamie *blows into his hands, presses his palms to his lips.*

Nina Darling? What are you doing?

Jamie Warming my lips.

And they kiss in the half light.

Int: **Nina***'s living room. Morning.*

Nina *and* **Jamie** *look out of the large window at the back of the house. They are playing the cloud game.*

They kneel on the sofa. **Nina***, as they characterise the clouds.*

Nina Australia!

Jamie Where?

Nina (*pointing*) There.

Jamie Good. (*Scours.*) Two lovers!

Nina Where?

Jamie (*pointing*) There. No arms, losing their legs, and . . . actually . . . becoming Europe.

Nina I can't see Europe.

Jamie Europe without Italy or Spain.

Nina That's hardly Europe. (*Of another.*) Your mother!

Jamie You think every cloud looks like my mother.

Nina This really does look like your mother. Look! Eyes, nose, the eyebrows, it's brilliant!

Jamie My mother has not got a beard.

Nina I see that as a sort of a – um ruffle.

They stare. They watch the clouds.

Nina *sings absently – snatches from Joni Mitchell's 'A Case of You'.*

Now **Jamie** *is joining in. They're hardly aware of singing.*

Then smiling, acknowledging the duet.

Nina I love you.

Jamie I love you.

Nina I really love you.

Jamie I really truly love you.

Nina I really truly madly love you.

Jamie I really truly madly deeply love you.

Nina I really truly madly deeply passionately love you.

Jamie I really truly madly deeply passionately remarkably love you.

Nina Remarkably?! Okay: I really truly madly deeply passionately remarkably deliciously love you.

Jamie I really truly madly passionately remarkably deliciously juicily love you.

Nina (*pouncing*) Deeply! Deeply! You passed on deeply! Which was your word, which means that you couldn't have meant it. You're a fraud. You're probably a figment of my imagination. And juicily!! Your forfeit. You play, I dance!

Nina *jumps off the sofa and dashes out of the living room.*

Jamie *closes the windows and looks at the clouds.*

Int: **Nina**'s *living room. Morning.*

Nina *dances, naked under* **Jamie**'s *coat.*

Jamie *plays a cello version of The Walker Brothers' 'The Sun Ain't Gonna Shine Anymore'.*

Very solemn. Both of them singing. He sings the words, she sings 'Jamie baby' at intervals.

Nina *goes to the piano to play the chorus.* **Jamie** *puts down his cello and jumps over the settee to join* **Nina** *at the piano. They sing the chorus together.*

The doorbell rings. They duck down under the piano.

Jamie I'll go.

He means he'll disappear.

Nina No. No.

They crawl to the window. **Nina** *looks out. It's* **Claire** *carrying a peace offering, a huge plant.*

Nina Oh, it's Claire.

Jamie She wanted my cello, didn't she? Bloody cheek!

Nina I want the world to go away.

Jamie Well, I don't know about the world, but I guarantee the rats have gone away.

Nina How?

Jamie Terrified of ghosts.

Nina Really?

Jamie Really. (*Looking out of the window.*) And now your sister's gone away too.

Claire and **Harry** *are going out of the front gate.*

Int: **Nina***'s bedroom. Morning.*

Nina*'s asleep.* **Jamie** *watching her.*

He's wearing his overcoat. He goes over to the bed, kneels down onto it, and begins, quirkily, to wake **Nina***. He sings into her ear, jiving a little.*

Jamie *sings, in passing imitation of Bob Dylan, from 'Tangled Up In Blue'.*

He's nuzzling her, she's trying to hide under a pillow.

Nina Ngggh. Go away.

Now it's Buddy Holly.

Jamie *sings from 'Raining In My Heart'.*

Jamie *picks up a glass and drips water onto* **Nina.**

Nina Oh God. I'm ill.

Jamie You're not ill.

Nina I'm sick.

Jamie You're not sick.

Nina I am sick, I've got tummy ache, I'm probably dying too. That'll be the next thing – I'll die as well.

Jamie *doesn't immediately respond.* **Nina***'s head pokes up from under the pillow.*

Nina Oh, sorry, sorry that was, I can't believe I said that.

Jamie I was wondering whether you were going to work today.

Nina No.

Jamie Okay.

Nina (*of dying*) I can't believe I just said that.

Jamie Don't worry.

The telephone rings. After four rings, the answer machine engages.

Jamie (*wry*) You should call in, so they know you're dying. They might be concerned.

Sandy (*on answer phone*) Nina. This is Sandy. Are you hibernating? Where are you?

Nina Do you think I should go in? Aren't you boiling?

Jamie I'm frozen, I've been trying to fix your central heating. Who put it in? It's unbelievable, what was wrong with thing, the guy, what was his name who did the shower at Coniston Road?

Nina It's working perfectly, it must be ninety degrees in here. Probably why I've got stomach ache. It's probably some tropical disease. I've probably got cholera, malaria! I can't go into work with malaria. Anyway . . . what would you do if I went to work?

Jamie Me? Don't worry about me, it's a time to catch up with a lot of things, I've been having Spanish lessons, I've been reading some very long . . .

Nina (*cutting in*) Spanish! I knew! I knew you had!

Jamie Oh?

Nina Because you were always, when I sensed you around, when I could sense you and feel you, and you were speaking, telling me to lock the back door you'd say, you'd say it in Spanish. And I was so, I was really, I was really touched that you . . . (*Can't resist.*) The accent's not great. But –

Jamie drags **Nina** off the bed and pushes her towards the living room.

She wanders through, looks at the number of messsages on the machine, frowns, then stumbles into the living room. Something has been changed.

Nina So I'm going in, am I? Oh, Jamie. What have you – what have –

Jamie comes through.

Jamie I changed a few things around. Tidied up a bit.

Nina (*interrupting*) Where's my tiger?

Jamie Better isn't it? (*Inquiring.*) I can change it back.

Nina No. No.

Jamie (*light*) You know I've got more sense of those things, you could never hang a picture, or – you know – could I light the fire?

Jamie *holds up a cloud mobile, which is tangled.*

Jamie I gave you this.

Nina I think I will have to go in, actually I can feel my face is hot.

Jamie Well, I've gotta be careful. Because you know I'm prone to colds, and, you imagine, I get a cold now it could last for ever.

Nina *laughs.* **Jamie** *doesn't.*

Jamie I'm not joking. I'm serious.

She looks at him. Considers.

Nina Thank you. (*Suddenly moved.*)

Jamie What for?

Nina Coming back.

Int: Translation office. Day.

It's a little like Babel as Chinese, Czech, French, Punjabi, Turkish, Greek, Italian leak from desk to desk.

People are here for immigration advice, for industrial translations, for medical interpretation, for help with letters to MPs, Local Authority communication, etc.

Members of staff work at terminals, doing postal translations or speak strange tongues into telephones. Exotic dictionaries abound.

Sandy *has a client who has bought a video machine and can't follow the instructions.*

Maura, *heavily pregnant, is carrying a black plastic bag across the room.*

Nina *comes in, rather furtively, carrying various items of translation work. Yellow stickers on the desk.*

Sandy *looks up from where he works.*

Nina (*to* **Translator**) Hi.

Sandy Nina!

Nina I'm sorry, I'm sorry, I'm sorry, I'm sorry, I'm sorry. (*She spots* **Maura**.) Maura, hello! Oh my God, is it Thursday?

Sandy It's Friday, Nina. Where've you been?

Titus *comes into the office, carrying a plank.*

Nina Titus, hello.

Titus (*straight-faced*) Hello.

Nina Maura, has she been, have you been here since yesterday? ¿Has estado aquí desde ayer?

Maura No, no.

Sandy She's doing some cleaning.

Nina What do you mean?

Sandy She's cleaning. We need someone, and she needs the money.

Nina Sandy, she's about to have a baby.

Sandy Excuse me, excuse me, could we just start all this again, please! You've disappeared off the face of the planet for a week, we have been working. You come back, we get told off.

To his French client, in English.

Sandy Sorry about this.

Frenchman Comment?

Sandy (*English*) I'll be with you in a minute.

Frenchman Comment?

Nina God, is it really Friday? My God.

Sandy Apart from anything else, Gabriella called me, and she was screaming and yelling and being hysterical, what else is new I know, but lucky for me Maura was here . . .

Nina How did that help?

Sandy Gabriella spoke to her, now Maura can speak to you . . . then you can speak to me.

Nina (*perplexed*) Oh, and what about Titus? Do we get all the ex-clients to come and work here now?

1. Juliet Stevenson as Nina, Vania Vilers as the Frenchman (left) and Bill Paterson as Sandy in the Translation Agency.

Photo: John Jefford © BBC Enterprises 1990

2. Juliet Stevenson as Nina (seated), Deborah Findlay as her sister Claire and Ian Hawkes as Harry (Nina's nephew and Claire's son).

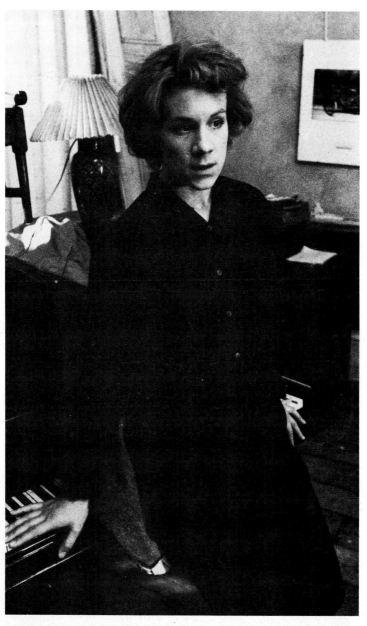

3. Juliet Stevenson as Nina.   Photo: Barry Boxall © BBC Enterprises 1990

4. Juliet Stevenson as Nina and Alan Rickman as Jamie.

Photo: Barry Boxall © BBC Enterprises 1990

5. The ghosts (including): Mark Long, Frank Baker, Teddy Kempner, Graeme Du-Fresne.

Photo: Barry Boxall © BBC Enterprises 1990

6. Michael Maloney as Mark and Juliet Stevenson as Nina.

Photo: Barry Boxall © BBC Enterprises 1990

7. Michael Maloney as Mark and Juliet Stevenson as Nina.

8. Alan Rickman as Jamie and other ghosts.

Photo: Barry Boxall © BBC Enterprises 1990

Sandy Excuse me.

Frenchman *anxious about the time.*

Frenchman Monsieur!

Sandy *without pausing for breath, but switching into French.*

Sandy Je sais, je sais. Vous devez prendre l'avion. (*Back to* **Nina** *and English.*) Well – what about an explanation, make something up . . . and why've you got the nerve to look so cheerful?

Nina That's a really tricky one, Sandy.

Sandy Yeah, I thought it might be.

Nina Do you love me?

Sandy No.

Nina No, I mean as a friend?

Sandy No.

Nina You do love me as a friend!

Sandy No, I don't.

Frenchman Je vous en prie, je dois aller à l'aeroport.

Sandy (*in French, hugely irritable*) Pourquoi vous n'avez pas acheter cet appareil en France?

Frenchman Je le demande.

Sandy (*to* **Nina**) And you'd better ring Rachel Reed . . .

Nina (*this is an interesting name for her*) Oh. Did she say what it was?

Sandy And I hope you're too late 'cause she rang on Monday. (*Straight back to the video manual.*) Maintenant, Monsieur. (*Reads.*) The fourteen day timer . . . (*Translates to French.*) La bouton programmation de quatorze jours.

Nina Sandy, I can tell you're forgiving me.

Sandy *doesn't pause, but glares affectionately at her. During this* **Titus** *walks by* **Nina**'s *desk on the way to the back of the office.*

Nina Are you okay?

Titus *shrugs miserably.*

Titus I come tonight, finish your cabinets?

Nina Well, tonight's not a good, it's not a . . .

Titus Okay, I come tomorrow.

Nina (*evasive*) Well, can we, can we talk about that tomorrow, can I telephone you?

Titus Sure.

Nina It's not that I don't want you to come and finish the, it's I've got some people staying at the moment, friends, and, they turned up unexpectedly, and –

Titus Okay.

He continues on his journey. With a heavy heart.

Nina *sits at her desk, moves the deluge of paper about for a few seconds. Sighs. The languages flow around her head.*

Titus *helps* **Maura** *carry a dustbin bag across the office.*

Ext: The park. Day.

Maura *and* **Nina** *walking. We see their reflection in the water.*

Nina How's the baby?

Maura Good. Very fine.

Nina Very fine's not, we don't say very fine, but I like it.

Maura How should I say?

Nina Very fine's fine.

Maura Tus amigos, Sandy y los otros, están muy preocupados por tí.

They walk up the steps.

Nina English, Maura.

Maura Oh, I can't.

Nina Yes, you can.

Maura Erm, Sandy, er, Titus, eh, very sad for you.

Nina Why are they sad for me?

Maura Because her man is dead.

Nina Your man. My man. Yes, well.

Maura I also sad.

Nina Maura, do you believe in life after death?

Maura *frowns, she doesn't understand.*

Nina ¿La vida después de la muerte, espíritus?

Maura ¿Espíritus? Sí, claro.

They walk along an arched walkway.

Maura Yo hice una película, un documentál en Chile, sobre fantasmas y – ¡claro que creo!

Nina You made a documentary?

Maura Sí, yo hago películas.

Nina Oh English, English.

Maura I make film. Many film. In Chile. In Chile I make film. In London I am cleaner. Ach!

She smiles. **Nina** *puts an arm through hers. They walk.*

Maura The spirits are everywhere. They are walking here with us.

Nina Oh yes.

They pass a tombstone with a statue of an angel on its side.

Int: Cafe in the park. Day.

Nina *and* **Maura** *come into the cafe. It's quiet. The odd pigeon from the park pecking at the entrance.*

Only one or two of the tables are occupied, mostly elderly Highgate intellectuals, but at one table, a youngish man sits, half-eating, half-absorbed, in a novel.

Maura *knows several of the waiters and waitresses who work at this cafe, including* **Roberto**. *She greets* **Roberto** *and they find a table.*

Roberto Hola Maura.

Maura (*to* **Nina** *as they sit down*) I was working here before.

Nina Oh did you? It's lovely.

Roberto *has come across, he embraces* **Maura**.

Roberto ¿Como estás?

Maura Bien, bien. Roberto, this is my friend, Nina. Nina, this is Roberto.

Nina Hello.

Roberto (*very warm, shaking her hand*) I am very pleased to meet you. Maura told us you help her.

Nina Oh, well.

Roberto (*to* **Maura**) Esperame un momento que yo regreso. ¿Café?

Maura Mm, café, sí.

Nina Yeah, coffee. Coffee's great. Thanks.

Roberto *goes off behind the counter.*

Nina Is Roberto from Chile?

Maura No, from El Salvador. He's a very good friend.

Nina Maura. You never told me who's the father of your baby? Is it Roberto?

Maura No, I think it is Wales man I met at Glastonbury Festival. I don't know. I try to find him. No problem. I want the baby.

Roberto *has reappeared with the coffees and a small case full of instruments. He sits down beside them and opens the case.*

Roberto There we are. Okay.

He produces an instrument for testing blood pressure and attaches it to Maura's arm.

Nina What's this? What's going on?

Maura Roberto is my doctor. I don't like hospitals.

Roberto (*by way of explanation*) I am doctor, was a doctor in my country. (*Reading the blood pressure.*) But I keep telling her she must go to the hospital, too. You tell her, she never listens to me.

Nina No. I have the same problem, Roberto.

Symonds (*OOV*) Roberto!

Maura Oh shit, the boss!

Symonds, *the owner, has emerged from the kitchen, looking thunderous.*

Symonds Roberto!

Roberto Just coming.

Symonds *comes over.*

Symonds What's going on here?

Roberto Nothing. I am just coming.

Symonds (*to* **Maura**) I might have known you'd be involved.

Maura *shrugs*.

Symonds (*to* **Nina**) Have you paid for these?

Nina We haven't had the bill yet.

Symonds (*sour*) Sure.

Nina I'm sorry?

Symonds Pull the other leg.

Nina What?

Symonds I've been looking at the till roll, looking at the bills, and counting the customers, and what do you know, they don't add up.

Maura ¡De nuevo otra vez!

Symonds I try to give you people a break. (*Hisses.*) It's a well known fact you're not meant to be working, but I don't ask any questions, and then, of course, I get diddled right under my nose.

Roberto I'm sorry, you speak too quickly.

Symonds I bet I do. Okay.

He looks round, a customer waits at the counter while a young waitress **Maura** *greeted when they came in, stands, transfixed by the confrontation.*

Symonds I'll say it in words of one syllable. You people have been ripping me off, stealing my money, stitching me up, robbing me? Comprenez?

Roberto (*gravely*) No!

Maura (*violent*) ¡El no te está robando, pero lo deberia hacer!

Roberto (*to* **Nina**) No nos ha pagado el sueldo que nos había prometido cuando nos contrató. Nos dijo cuatro libras, pero nada más que nos ha pagado tres libras porque dice que no pagamos impuestos en este país.

Symonds Can anybody speak the Queen's English here?

Nina I can. This man is saying you've been cheating him and all the other employees.

Symonds I bloody well have not.

Roberto Asi que tenemos un arreglo entre nosotros. Por cada hora que trabajamos cogemos una libra. Por ejemplo, no registramos el dinero de los cafés. Pero nunca cogemos más que esta libra que ves.

Symonds (*over this*) I bloody well have not been cheating them. I'm telling you, they're lucky I give them work, they're all here illegally. I can tell you that for nothing!

Nina (*to* **Symonds**) Can you shut up a minute! Okay. He's saying you promised them all four pounds an hour . . . which is pretty criminal, incidentally . . . and then you dock them a pound of that on some specious basis.

Symonds They're not paying tax! They come here and sponge off – 'cause I'm paying tax, I'm not exempt –

Nina (*interrupting*) I'd be very interested to know their legal position, anyway, what they're doing is paying themselves the extra pound, which is their money, by not ringing up the coffees, seems to make perfect sense to me.

Symonds (*over this*) Don't tell me about their legal position –

Roberto (*over this*) ¡Debíamos mandar a este cabrón a mi país. Le cortarían los cojones!

Symonds (*over this*) – 'Cause I could make one telephone call, and these lot would be down the police station! (*Turning on* **Roberto**.) I heard that, calling me a bastard! Don't think I don't understand a lot of what you're saying!

He shoves **Roberto**. **Roberto** *shoves him back. He shoves* **Roberto**, *who falls against the table. It's not funny.*

Nina (*flashing with anger*) Come on. Watch it.

During this, **Mark**, *the young man with the meal and the novel, has been watching events with interest. He suddenly stands up.*

Mark (*a huge distraction*) There is nothing up my left sleeve! There is nothing up my right sleeve! There is nothing on my plate except gravy. (*Traces the plate then licks his fingers.*) Yum. I take this novel, Russian, it must always be a Russian novel, and I throw it in the air.

He does so. As it flies from his hands it becomes a pigeon which flutters, anxious, then flaps out for freedom.

Roberto ¡Increíble!

Mark (*a slight bow*) Any chance of another coffee?

Ext: Street. Day.

Nina *and* **Maura** *approach.* **Mark**'s *car is parked. He gets out.*

Mark (*from the car*) Would you like a lift?

Nina We're fine, I think. Maura?

Maura Sí, claro.

Nina Thanks, anyway. And thanks, thanks for your performance, for intervening back there. It was pretty extraordinary.

Mark (*making light of it*) Any excuse.

Nina Is that your profession?

Mark Magic? Oh no. No, no it's not. Uh . . .

He seems about to say something else.

Nina What?

Mark Nothing. Right, okay.

Nina Bye.

He closes the passenger door and goes round to get into the driver's seat.

Nina *watches him, her interest tugged.*

Maura (*appreciatively, of* **Mark**) Very fine person!

Ext: **Nina**'s *building. Early evening.*

As **Nina** *arrives home, laden up with stuff from work,* **George** *emerges from his van. Not quite what* **Nina** *had in mind.*

George I'd been calling and calling.

Nina George, hello.

George Is that answer-machine working? Thought I'd better come round.

Nina Oh dear, and have you been waiting?

George I was getting a bit worried about you.

Nina I'm fine.

George (*busy organising himself*) Still bad in there, is it?

Nina What?

George In the flat . . .

Does a little scurrying mime along the front bonnet.

Nina George, George, George, you're not going to believe this –
they've gone.

George Well, of course, they won't have gone, but good, good.

Nina No, no, they've definitely gone. It's amazing.

George Nina, ask me how many years I've been in Pest Control . . .
and shall I tell you, like all wars, you develop a healthy respect for
the enemy. Never underestimate him.

He's at the back of the van, getting out his suitcase and plastic gloves.

George A rat is a highly intelligent creature, he's a formidable
opponent.

Nina (*awkward*) George, actually this is a really bad time, George.
It's not a good time.

George It's no problem. I don't need to stop. Five minutes in and
out. That car's been here yonks. I've told you. It's gotta go. What's
the matter?

Nina Nothing, nothing, nothing. Come in, of course. I'll make you a
cup of tea. I'll just – er . . .

She rings the bell to her own front door, long and hard.

Nina (*turning, shrugging to* **George**) I always do that. Frighten off the
ghosts.

And they go in.

Int: **Nina***'s flat. Front door to kitchen corridor to bathroom corridor to kitchen.
Evening.*

The front door opens, **Nina** *comes in,* **George** *shuffling behind her. She is not
really listening to* **George** *as she scours the flat for* **Jamie***, whispering
'Jamie' under her breath.*

In passing she notes yet more alterations to the flat.

George They lie low . . .

Nina Jamie.

George No, it's quite astonishing, they lie low, they won't touch the trays . . . So I clear off, and then they come back. They're not stupid.

Nina No, no.

George No, no you see your trays are untouched. Your trays are untouched.

Nina Mm.

George You know, I think they talk to each other.

Nina Jamie.

Nina*'s gone from room to room. Nothing.*

George (*approaching*) You've had a tidy up.

Nina Yeah, (*Shrugs.*) well, it needed it.

George He's got a soft spot for you, you know.

Nina (*rather alarmed*) Who?

George (*explaining*) Titus. I've always been rather fond of the Poles, myself.

Nina Let me make the tea.

George Lovely. Is it me or is it very hot in here?

Int: **Nina***'s bedroom. Evening.*

George *knocks on and peers round the door.*

George That's me. I'm off.

Nina All right, George. Thanks for coming. And, sorry if I was a bit unwelcoming.

George You're a lovely girl.

Nina *smiles.*

George I was telling my wife all about you.

Nina (*very surprised*) Oh? Really? George, I'm sorry – I thought your wife had died.

George (*nodding*) 1978. Still talk to her though. Tell her my day. Don't you do that?

Nina I do, yes.

George 'And death shall have no dominion.' We know that, you and me, eh?

Int: **Nina***'s bathroom. Evening.*

Nina *is in the bath. She's finished her ablutions. She is wearing a face pack.*

She hums. It's a very private moment.

A toy dolphin appears by **Nina***'s face. It eats the fish on a string.*

Nina God!

Jamie*'s face appears over the side of the bath.*

Jamie Hi.

Nina *is absolutely shaken to find* **Jamie** *sitting at the edge of the tub.*

Nina Don't do that! You scared me half to – ! Don't ever do that!

Jamie Is this a bad time?

Nina *leaning back in the bath.*

Nina It's a terrible time, Jamie. There are some things . . .

Jamie Oh, come on, don't be coy.

Nina I'm serious! Go away!

Jamie Darling, I knew you shaved your legs.

Nina, *appalled at the epiphany that locked doors have no meaning any more.*

Nina God, I can't even lock the door on you any more!

Jamie I thought you might be pleased to see me.

Nina No, I'm not.

Jamie *sulks. She scoops some bubbles out of the bath and puts them on his nose.*

Nina Yes, I am pleased, but just leave me alone for a bit. Of course I'm pleased to see you. I was terrified you'd gone.

They kiss.

Jamie See you later.

Nina Yep.

Jamie *goes to the door. It's locked.*

Jamie Why do you lock this?

Nina I don't know.

He's unlocked the door. As it opens, distant hubbub appears to be coming from another room.

Nina Have you turned the telly on?

Jamie (*uncomfortable*) Uh, yes. Um. Listen, sweetheart, don't get, but some of the guys wanted to come back and, just watch a couple of videos.

Nina What guys?

Jamie Friends, some friends . . .

Nina Dead friends?

Jamie (*casually*) I don't know, I suppose so, yes.

Nina Are you telling me there are dead people in my living room watching videos?

Jamie *shrugs.*

Nina (*irritated*) Well, I mean. Aren't there videos available wherever they are normally?

Jamie (*haughty*) Look if it's a problem, these are my friends, Nina, no, okay, I'll send them away, sure.

Nina No, it's fine. It's absolutely fine.

Jamie I'd forgotten you could be like this.

Nina Be like what?

Jamie Doesn't matter.

Nina I said it's fine.

Jamie *sneezes.*

Nina Bless you.

Jamie *sneezes.*

Nina Bless you.

Jamie (*is this a cold coming!*) Oh no.

He exits. A third sneeze. **Nina** *frowns, sinks back into the bath.*

Int: **Nina***'s flat – bathroom to hall to living room. Night.*

Four men are lounging male-like around the television, various ages, their antecedents hard to identify. They all wear warm coats. One of them, **Isaac***, is talking about the film 'Easy Street' which they are watching.*

Nina *emerges from the bathroom, wrapped in a robe, and comes – apprehensively – into the living room.*

Jamie *gets up as* **Nina** *enters.*

Jamie Oh, Nina. This is Freddie and this is Pierre. This is Bruno. And this is –

Isaac Isaac.

Nina Hello.

Jamie Isaac. This is Nina.

Muted, polite hello's.

Nina (*awkward*) Well, can I get anybody anything?

Muted, polite no's.

Bruno The tape with 'Manhattan' written on it – it isn't.

Nina Oh no, you know, the other day I was trying to record 'Hannah and Her Sisters' . . .

Bruno It's a lovely film.

Nina . . . on the end and I think, I've got a terrible feeling – (*Turns to* **Jamie**.) I'm so hopeless with that machine.

Jamie You haven't recorded over it! Nina . . . ! (*To the others.*) She did that with 'Strangers on a Train'!

Bruno Really? What a drag!

Isaac I love 'Strangers on a Train'.

So do the others.

Freddie He's wonderful in that, isn't he?

Isaac Fantastic.

Nina Sorry.

Bruno That's such a drag.

Nina Sorry.

Jamie *puts a finger to her temple like a pistol and pulls the trigger.*

Int: **Nina**'s *living room. Night.*

Later. And 'Brief Encounter' is finishing on the television. The ghosts are moved. They share blankets and Kleenex in the darkened room.

Nina's *asleep on the settee.* **Jamie** *next to her.*

Isaac *jumps up.*

Isaac Okay, 'Five Easy Pieces' or 'Fitzcarraldo'?

Various voices. **Nina** *wakes up.*

Nina Guys, guys. Actually, I'm going to have to go to bed.

A muted chorus of goodnights. **Jamie** *kisses* **Nina**.

Jamie I'll be in in a minute.

Nina (*to* **Jamie**) Don't be long.

Isaac (*on the next film*) Let's take a vote.

Int: **Nina**'s *bedroom. Night.*

Jamie *stumbles into the bedroom and clambers into the bed. He rescues the pile of quilts which have fallen onto the floor.*

Jamie (*sliding against* **Nina**) Mmm, you smell so nice.

Nina (*asleep but agreeable*) Nnngggh.

Jamie Were you asleep?

Nina Nnngggh.

They snuggle up.

Jamie Nina, have we still got that hot water bottle?

Nina Oh, Jamie, the thing is I'm so hot, I'm suffocating, I'm too hot.

Jamie Okay, don't worry, don't worry, I love you, sshhh, go back to sleep.

He sneezes.

Jamie The guys are nice, aren't they?

Nina Nnnghhh.

He sneezes.

Jamie Great guys.

Ext: Bus stop on London street. Day.

Nina *waiting for a bus to go to* **Burge** – *her therapist's – house.*

The bus draws up. A group of mentally handicapped teenagers and young adults start to get off the bus. Showing the way is **Mark**. **Anthony**, *one of the group, is getting off as* **Nina** *gets on to the bus.*

Nina *sees* **Mark** *and greets him. She's pleased to see him again.*

Nina Oh, hi.

Mark, *delighted to see her.*

Mark Hello!

Nina How are you?

Mark Fine, fine. This is Anthony. Anthony, this is my friend uh –

Nina Nina.

Mark Nina.

Anthony Hello Nina.

Nina Hello.

Mark We're going for a walk, we're going to do some painting and have a picnic.

Anthony Do you want to come?

Nina Uh . . .

Mark I think Nina's probably busy.

Nina No, actually I'd like to, I'd love to, but I, I've got an appointment. I'm late.

Mark Well, nice to see you.

Anthony *knows the catchphrase.*

Anthony To see you nice!

Nina Yeah. You too.

Mark How's your friend, by the way, who's having the baby?

Nina Oh, Maura? She's fine, fine . . .

Mark, *suddenly aware that his group is dispersing.*

Mark No, don't disappear. Helen! Adrian! Just – (*He turns to* **Nina**.) I'd better go.

Nina Okay. Okay. Bye.

Mark *and his group head off up a path.* **Nina** *goes to sit on the bus.*

Mark (*OOV*) Nina! Nina!

Nina *stands up.* **Mark** *has come back to the side of the bus.*

Mark Sorry.

Nina *winds down the window.*

Mark Look, uh, I was wondering, do you think maybe sometime we could, this is probably terrible, you say no but –

Nina Yes, I'd like to.

Mark (*delighted, surprised*) Oh, really!

Nina Yes.

Mark Well, can I call you?

Nina Uh, yes. No. No, no, I'll call you.

Mark (*disappointed*) Okay.

Nina No, I will call, it's just, have you got a pen?

Mark Yeah. I think so. No. Don't go away.

He sprints back to his group. By this time **Mark**'s *whole party have assembled to watch the proceedings. They smile at* **Nina**.

Mark *gets a pen and hares back to* **Nina**.

Mark I haven't got any paper.

Nina, *holds her hand out of the bus window.*

Nina Doesn't matter. Write on that.

Mark 261 0840. Or you can get me at work. 267 – I can't remember.

Nina That's fine.

Mark 'Bye.

Nina 'Bye.

He goes back to the good-natured observations of his charges. **Mark** *waves. The whole group waves.*

Int: **Burge**'s *office. Day.*

Nina *on the settee.*

Nina I was reading, uh. I was reading and must have been one of those books you lent me on, about bereavement, and it was about how it's possible some people might get this sen – this powerful sensation that their loved one has come back, I don't mean like a *sense* of their presence – an abstract thing. I mean, you know, they they've *actually come back* and are in their house. Well, what do you think about that? Is that ridiculous?

There is a long pause.

Burge What? Is what ridiculous?

Nina I don't know, that . . . well, when I read this, I thought – how ridiculous! I mean –

Burge Why?

Music: Bach: Brandenburg No 3, 1st Movement.

Nina Well, no, I can imagine it. I mean, I can imagine going home this evening and there's Jamie. And he's back –

Burge (*prompting*) All right.

Nina – but then, but then what?

Int: **Nina**'s *living room. Night.*

Nina *kneels at the open window. The music swells.*

Burge (*VO*) What you are saying is ridiculous?

Nina, *dizzy with her predicament.*

Nina (*VO*) Well – oh, I don't know, I don't know, everything, everything, everything. I don't know. I don't know.

Nina *closes the window and sits down to reveal* **Jamie**, *and a dozen other musicians, giving a performance of the Bach Brandenburg.*

Nina *is concentrating, moved, but tight, feeling claustrophobic.*

There are a dozen other members of the audience scattered around the room, on the floor, squashed on the settee, including **Isaac**, **Bruno** *and* **Freddie**.

Apart from the overcoats and scarves it could be a neo-Victorian Chamber Evening.

Jamie *catches* **Nina***'s eye. Smiles. She smiles back, tries to look calm, but she's in turmoil.*

The music soars.

Ext: The south bank. Early evening.

The river. **Mark** *is waiting patiently for* **Nina** *– who, late, hurrying, finally turns up.*

Nina (*as she approaches*) I'm sorry, I'm sorry, I'm sorry. Oh God. I'm so sorry.

Mark, *ever the magician, pulls a bunch of blood red roses from his jacket.*

Mark (*with a flourish*) Madam.

Then flinching, as if from the thorns, and feeling inside his shirt.

Mark Ouch. Sorry –

Nina Oh, they're glorious, thank you, they're, the scent!

Then, of their date – they were off to the National Theatre.

Nina I'm sorry, I know it's ridiculously, it's started hasn't it, but I –

Mark (*calming*) It doesn't matter. We can do something else.

Nina No, I can't. I can't.

Mark Why? Has something happened?

Nina I have to be somewhere else. It's very complicated.

Mark (*now openly deflated*) Okay.

Nina No, listen. It's complicated but not for, I guarantee whatever you're thinking is not why it's complicated. Truly.

Mark What am I going to tell my group? They're on tenterhooks.

Nina Is that, is – are they your work?

Mark (*by way of saying yes*) We were drawing trees, you know, you draw a tree and then you draw in the roots and the branches and you put in all the names which are important, have you got time for this?

Nina Of course, sure, I just haven't –

Mark, *he's drawing an imaginary tree.*

Mark Okay, you draw a tree and then on the roots of the tree you put the people who were important in forming you, or stabilising you, or taking care of you . . . Mum, Dad, sister . . . whoever, and then you put in the names of people who are around you now and – this is on the branches, like leaves. Sorry, are you with me?

Nina Yes, I think so.

Mark And I did, I was painting my own tree, and Anthony, who you met, Anthony was looking at my tree and he suddenly said, *well where's Nina*? Actually, it's not just my group who's on tenterhooks, but, anyway can I give you a lift?

Nina No, really. I'll be fine.

Mark Aren't we both going north? I could just drop you at the end of the road. It would be –

Nina I'll get a bus. Really. It's better if I – You can walk me to the Underground . . . if you want . . .

They walk in silence. Then after a while.

Mark (*attempting to see the funny side*) This is my shortest ever date. Yours?

Nina Yes.

Mark That's something, then. (*Dry.*) Are you interested in my last name? Or – no, no, hang on – stop!

Nina What?

He stops her and maps out a course.

Mark Okay. Okay. Look, this is what we do. I tell you everything about my life between here and that statue there. See it? . . . we hop of course . . . and then you tell me everything about yours. No lies from the speaker, no interruptions, no questions from the listener. And I'm off:

He hops, he begins at full tilt.

Mark Mark Damian de Grunwald, born Budleigh Salterton, 32 next birthday, Capricorn, don't believe in that – that's star signs I mean, parents alive, retired, father silent practically completely silent, eighteen years older than my mother who is not, completely silent, owned a mill, then a post office, then a tea shop, amateur magician, father that is, and I was his assistant at Conservative Club Dinner Dances, regularly sawn in half from the age of seven, and made to disappear in ideologically unsound circumstances. Change legs. What else? Home: okay, puberty: okay, parents: okay, one brother:

okay, academically: okay, vaguely asthmatic attempted suicide at seventeen, can't remember why, I was sad about something, aspirins, stomach pump, followed by weekly sessions with educational psychologist for whom I developed an enormous passion and encouraged me to become a psychologist myself, A levels, Psychology degree at Sussex University, trained in Art Therapy, what is Art Therapy? You draw trees. Have one daughter, Gemma, seven, that should come earlier, uh, lived with Gemma's mother for three weeks before she left me for theology student, I've stopped believing in God, but long enough with me to get pregnant. Gemma is seven, did I say that already? And her hair is curly and has red sparks, you know, in the sun, and she calls me Mark de Grunwald and the vicar she calls Daddy and –

The statue looms.

Mark I love, basically everything – you know: music, curry, I can practically recite the collected works of

A few hops from the statue.

Mark Oh hello. And I live alone and my fridge is empty and I wash my own clothes and I'm interested in Nina who is not on my tree and I can do magic. And now you go. And straight away. Yes. Don't think. Go!

Nina *looks at him. She likes, is confused, intrigued by this biographical sketch. She hesitates.*

Nina (*wavering*) I can't.

Mark Yes.

Nina Er –

And she plunges in.

Nina Nina Mitchell –

Mark (*interrupting*) You've got to hop, you've got to hop!

She hops.

Nina Nina Mitchell, I can't believe I'm doing this! Also Capricorn, but also don't believe so I can't make anything of that, think there may be a God, interpreter, I'm starting at the end, I believe in protesting, in the possibility of change, in making this planet more, decent. You know, you see it all the time. I hate what this country is doing to itself, and to the people, and the way we treat other races, visitors, this happens every day . . . well you know, you saw it in the cafe . . . wrong skin, wrong size, wrong shape: you're lost . . . or wrong religion, wrong ideology, wrong class, it makes me so! Oh, do you want me to be more personal? Um, okay, parents alive, Gloucestershire, teachers, him Geography, her History, so holidays it would be *Dad, where are we? Mum, have we been here before?* I like them, I have a sister, Claire, I love her, she has a family and a husband I can't stand who keeps climbing everything – climbs socially, in business, and now – finally – has started climbing mountains. Um, they have a son, Harry. She's pregnant again for the second time, their son is my nephew, and I adore him. Did I say I was born in Stratford? Well, I was and do you know that I pay to do this once a week, to talk, that's where I was going the other day when I saw you on the bus, to my woman, the Burge, Doctor Burge. The only difference is there you get fifty minutes and no exercise and here it seems to spill out, and I play the piano, I love Bach, I have rats, I'm in a mess, I live alone, I haven't always, not always –

There is a busker playing. The music pulls her as she talks, he's playing one of the Bach Sarabands.

Something causes **Nina** *to turn and look. It's* **Jamie***! She stops, dumbfounded.*

Mark Hey! Come on Nina. You're not hopping. Come on.

Nina*, oblivious, has turned and walked towards the busker. It's not* **Jamie***.*

Nina *watches for a few seconds.*

Ext: **Nina***'s street and house. Night.*

As **Nina** *approaches, she can hear* **Jamie** *practising his cello in the living room. She loves him, feels badly. She has the roses with her. She dumps them into a rubbish bin.*

Int: **Nina***'s living room. Night.*

Nina *comes in.* **Jamie** *stops playing. It is the Bach Saraband.*

Nina (*genuine*) I love you. Don't stop.

Jamie (*gently*) Where've you been?

Nina Nowhere, nowhere, work.

Jamie You're so late.

Nina I know. Sorry.

Jamie I got worried.

Nina Sorry.

Jamie (*wry*) Just like old times.

Nina *and* **Jamie** *consider each other. The room seems large without the crew of spirits.*

Jamie Is there something you want to tell me?

Nina I have this feeling you're with me, are you with me all day?

Jamie No.

Nina I think of you as being on my shoulder, and if you're there, then you'll know I am like someone who carries their loved one on their shoulder . . . if that was what you were asking . . .

Jamie I'm not, but thank you.

Nina Excuse me, where is my television? And the video machine!

Jamie Oh, right, I put them in our bedroom because people couldn't get comfortable in here, it's so cold in the evenings, and, and anyway I wanted to play and – don't worry they'll move when we want to go to bed, it's no problem, don't get frazzled.

Nina (*frustrated*) Oh please.

Jamie Nina, you can't come home in the middle of the night and then complain I've got company.

Nina It's not the middle of the night! I don't know these people. I don't know, I don't even know what period they're from. This is ridiculous!

Jamie You could try talking to them.

Nina I can't believe this is happening! I've got ghosts watching videos in my bedroom and I'm being accused – of what? What am I being accused of? Jamie, they're dead people! The rats have gone, now I'm infested with ghosts!

Jamie There are eight or nine people in there, they're not doing you any harm. If you want to go to bed, they'll go. Just tell them. If you want me to go, just tell me.

Nina And why are they all men! I don't want you to go, darling. I don't want you to go! I don't know what I want. Anyway, I bought you a hot water bottle. Do you want it?

She pulls a hot water bottle out of her bag. It's shaped like a pig. **Jamie** *inspects it. He's pleased.*

Jamie Thanks. It's great.

He comes behind her and puts his arms round her.

Nina I mean, why can't you go back to, to Heaven! while I'm at work?

Jamie I don't know. It's like you make a choice and then you, I don't know. I'm here. It's fine. It's fine. I love you.

He scrapes his cheek against her.

Jamie Smooth?

They laugh. **Freddie***'s head comes round the door.*

Freddie Hello Nina, I thought I heard you, did you remember to go to the – ?

The sound of 'The Lavender Hill Mob' comes from the bedroom.

Nina *rummaging, pulling out videos.*

Nina They didn't have 'I Vitelloni' but I got 'Pinocchio' and 'Forget Venice'.

Freddie Fantastic! Have you seen that, Jamie? 'Forget Venice'? Fantastic. So tender. By the way Isaac says you're in check. It's your move. It looks bad.

Jamie (*getting up*) I can't be! How can I be in check? Hang on a second sweetheart.

And **Jamie***'s off.* **Nina** *sits on the arm of the settee. She leans across and plucks the strings of the cello.*

Int: **Nina***'s hall. Night.*

It's the middle of the night and the telephone is ringing.

Nina *stumbles into the corridor.*

Freddie, *sleeping nearest to the telephone, picks up the receiver, doesn't answer it, but holds it out, frowning with sleep, to* **Nina**, *who trips over a sleeping body or two on her way to the receiver.*

Nina *winces, a kicked body groans and turns over.*

Nina Oh. Sorry. Thanks, Freddie. (*Into receiver.*) Oh God. Hello, yeah. Yeah. Okay. Of course. Yeah, I'll come.

She's learning that **Maura** *has gone prematurely into labour and that she's given the hospital admin.* **Nina***'s name as next of kin.*

Int: Maternity side room. Night.

Maura *is in a side room prior to going into a delivery room. The* **Midwife** *is with her.*

Nina *hurries in to her.*

Nina Maura, querida.

Maura Hola. Gracias por venir. Perdona la hora, pero la guagua está a punto de llegar.

Nina No, está bien, está bien. ¿Cómo estás? Yo estoy contentísima, emocionada. ¿Y tú?

Maura Estoy muerta de miedo.

Nina Yo tambien. Me han dicho que todo esta bien.

Maura *gets a contraction. She squeezes* **Nina***'s hand.*

Nina Hello, I'm Maura's friend. How is she?

Midwife She's fine. She'll be going in to the delivery room any minute.

Maura ¡Ven conmigo!

Nina She wants me to come with her, can I?

Midwife I don't see why not.

Nina Is everything, everything is, is it all – ?

Midwife Don't worry.

Nina Oh! Listen. Excuse me. Have you talked to her about medication, because, I mean have you given her any drugs or what?

Midwife She hasn't had anything yet. She can have gas and air, or pethidine, or whatever she wants.

Nina Hang on, can I just check with her, because I don't think that. (*Switching in mid-breath.*) Oye Maura, ¿quieres un calmante? Te van a ofrecer unas drogas para el dolor, ¿las quieres?

Maura Yes. Drugs. Give me drugs!

Nina (*a little deflated*) Well she thinks she does, at the moment, you know, but –

Maura *is crying.*

Nina Hey, what's the matter? ¿Qué te pasa?

Maura Titus. Yo quiero que Titus esté aquí también.

Nina ¿Quién? Perdona Maura, ¿quién?

Maura Titus. Yo quiero que Titus esté aquí.

Nina (*taken aback*) ¿Titus? ¿De verdad? Bueno . . .

Midwife Titus, yes, she's said that name several times. Is that the father?

Maura Titus me ama. Te lo quería contar, pero no te he visto.

Nina He loves you? Oh, does he? That's nice.

Midwife Okay, we can go in now.

Maura Titus. Quiero que venga. Quiero que venga. Titus. Titus. Titus.

Maura *is wheeled off, calling for* **Titus**.

Int: Delivery room. Early dawn.

Titus *and* **Nina** *encourage* **Maura** *over the final hurdles. It's all happening. Triumph on three faces.*

Int: Side ward. Early dawn.

Titus *is asleep beside* **Maura**.

Maura *has been feeding her baby. She hands her over to* **Nina**.

Nina Qué linda, qué linda, qué linda. (*Tearful.*) A new life, a new life. Hello. Hello, darling.

She kisses the **Baby**'s *forehead.*

Nina A new life.

Int: **Nina**'s *hall. Day.*

As **Nina** *lets herself into the flat,* **Freddie** *and another ghost are dragging a bookcase into an already crowded hallway.*

Nina What's going on?

Freddie Hi Nina . . . (*To the other ghost, managing the manoeuvre.*) Just hang on a minute.

They set the bookcase down with a grunt. **Freddie** *dusts down his hands.*

Freddie So tell me, was it a boy or a girl?

Nina Girl.

Freddie (*excited*) A girl! It was a girl! (*Calling.*) Pierre? Pierre!

Pierre *appears.*

Freddie Maura had a little girl.

Pierre (*thrilled*) Tremendous.

Freddie (*to* **Nina**) Was it moving? Isn't birth moving?

Nina Freddie, what's going on with the furniture?

Freddie Oh, it's going to be great. Jamie took a look at the floorboards in there and they're fabulous, they're beautiful, they're those Victorian boards, we're just getting the carpet – even as we speak!

Nina *goes past* **Freddie** *and negotiates the obstacle course to the door to the living room.*

Int: **Nina***'s living room. Day.*

Nina *enters just in time to see the carpet roll by her feet, pushed by* **Jamie** *and company.*

Jamie Hi! (*To his crew.*) Good work.

Kneeling to inspect the revealed floorboards.

Jamie We just need to scrub this up a bit. It's oak. Is it oak?

Isaac It's definitely a hard wood.

Jamie – or ash?

Nina (*absolutely exasperated*) Jamie, what are you doing?

Jamie Aren't these boards amazing? Who would have thought under that disgusting carpet . . . you need to burn it by the way . . . it's full of mildew and silverfish, but these boards! So, it was a girl.

Nina I liked that carpet.

Jamie Don't be perverse.

Nina Well, I did like it and you can't just go around pulling, treating my flat as –

Jamie Nina, the carpet was threadbare, it is threadbare, and it's full of mould and mildew and . . . and these boards, even you must acknowledge that, these are in a different – !

Nina (*raging*) I feel like I'm being burgled! Every time I come home I feel like I've been burgled!

Jamie What?

He frowns at the others.

Nina (*flailing*) Oh God. The flat – chairs are moved! The the the . . . pictures are different, they're not where, and, it's my flat! It's my flat! I mean – !

Jamie Do you want to have a row in public? It's actually quite embarrassing for everybody . . . for me . . . and uh . . .

He turns and shrugs to his mates.

Nina Well no, I don't, no I don't want to be in public in my own home. That's right. That's absolutely right! So, in fact, could your friends go, please, could everybody just go, do you think? Is that possible? That I could have some time in my, now! Now! Please. Is that, is that asking too much?

Jamie (*to his cronies*) Sorry.

*The **Ghosts** leave, rather sulkily. **Nina** and **Jamie** alone.*

Jamie (*furious*) Satisfied?

Then he sneezes, dramatically, repeatedly.

Nina (*acidly*) It's only dust.

Jamie Nina, that was really humiliating. You ask people to give you a hand, they don't need to, they lug your furniture around half the day and then you come back and throw a tantrum. That was really really really humiliating.

He sneezes again. It settles in silence.

Nina (*desperate, floundering*) Was it like this before?

Jamie (*as he blows his nose*) What?

Nina Before, were we like this?

Jamie What? Like what? Look, you're tired, your friend just had a baby, you were up half the night, it's traumatic, it's an emotional experience, let's not turn that into –

Nina Tell me about the first night we spent together.

Jamie Why? Seriously? You want me to?

Nina What did we do?

Jamie We talked.

Nina What else?

Jamie Well, talking was the major component! Uh, uh, we, you played the piano – and I played and we both played a duet – something, I can't remember . . . and you danced for about three hours until I fell asleep, but you were fantastic! – and then we had some cornflakes and when we kissed – which was about eleven o'clock the following day – we were trembling so much we couldn't take off our clothes.

They remember. They're both sitting now on the bare boards. Quiet. Closer.

Nina You see, I held that baby – so

She makes a tangible gesture.

It's life, it's a life I want. And, and, and all my taste . . . my things, after you died. I found stuff in my trunk I'd put there because you disapproved or laughed at them – books and photographs and I couldn't, I didn't know how to mend a fuse or find a plumber or bleed a radiator but – and now I do. It is a ridiculous flat, but I'll get there, it'll be beautiful, it could be, I think it could be. I, I, I – I so much longed for you, I longed for you.

Jamie How's your Spanish?

Nina What?

Jamie There's a poem I wanted you to translate. I read it, there's a bit that I wanted to tell you, I wanted you to hear –

Nina Okay.

Jamie *recites an extract from the poem, 'The Dead Woman' by Pablo Neruda.*

Jamie Uh – Perdóname.

Nina *(translating)* Forgive me . . .

Jamie Si tú no vives,

Nina I know this poem. If you are not living . . .

Jamie Si tú, querida, amor mío,
Si tu te has muerto

Nina If you, beloved, my love,
If you have died

Jamie Todas las hojas caerán en mi pecho

Nina All the leaves will fall on my breast

Jamie Lloverá sobre mi alma noche y día

Nina It will rain on my soul, all night, all day

Jamie Mis piés querrán marchar hacia donde tú duermes

Nina My feet will want to march to where you are sleeping
Your accent's terrible.

Jamie Pero seguiré vivo

Nina *gets up and goes to* **Jamie**.

Nina My feet will want to march to where you are sleeping but I
shall go on living.

Jamie Do you want me to go?

She clings to him.

Nina No, never, never, never, never, never.

Ext: Outside **Nina**'s *flat. Day.*

Nina *comes out of the flat.*

Int: **Nina**'s *living room. Day.*

Jamie *is still sitting on the floor of the living room. The others pile in.*

Freddie (*apprehensive*) Well?

Jamie *shrugs, gives them a sad smile.*

Jamie I think so, yes.

Freddie's kind compassionate smile.

Ext: Bridge. Day.

Nina *walks across the bridge.*

Ext: Cafe. Day.

Nina *sits at a table outside the cafe with a cup of coffee.*

Ext: Mental Handicap Centre. Day.

Nina *makes her way into the building where* **Mark** *works.*

Inside she sees **Mark** *with his group. There's some sort of activity going on.* **Nina** *finds their movements simple, uncluttered – intolerably moving.*

Mark *spots her, comes to the window. He's a little wary. He looks at her. She shrugs. She beams and mimes incomprehensibly. He beams and mimes incomprehensibly.*

Then **Anthony** *and the others come to the window. They wave.* **Nina** *waves back.*

Ext: Mental Handicap Centre car park. Day.

Mark *and* **Nina** *make their way towards his car.*

Mark We could see a film.

Nina Okay.

Mark (*wry*) Or we could try the play again?

Nina Okay.

Mark Or we could, we could just go home and eat.

Nina (*benign*) Anything.

They've reached the car. He opens her door and goes round to open his door. **Nina** *leans against the door and starts to cry.* **Mark** *goes round to her.*

Nina I'm sorry, I'm going to cry, and it's not going to make any sense and I feel really . . . I'm so sorry.

Mark I've sort of worked out you're living with somebody, I mean I'm not a private detective but you won't tell me where you live, you won't give me your number, so –

Nina No, I'm not, I'm really not living with anybody.

Mark You know, because if you're, if you're not free I think – because to be quite honest I'm in trouble here.

He means he's hooked.

Mark I'm, I could embarrass myself.

Nina I think I am free. I did love someone very much, you see. Very much. But he died. He died. And I've found it quite hard to get over it.

Mark Well, why don't we just go home? If you want you could talk, you can tell me whatever, anything, everything.

Nina Okay. Yeah.

They get into the car.

Ext.:/Int: **Mark**'s *car. Night.*

Mark's *car goes across the bridge.*

They're driving. They're squeezed up together, very close, smiling.

Nina (*suddenly*) Oh, could you stop, could you stop? Please. Stop.

Mark Sh, sure.

Mark *stops the car. He looks really deflated.*

Mark Are you all right?

Nina *dashes from the car, leaves her door swinging. We don't go with her, but stay on* **Mark**'s *disappointment. He thumps the steering wheel in frustration and then she's suddenly jumping back into the car.*

Nina Okay.

Mark What was all that about?

He looks perplexed. She holds up a toothbrush in its packet.

Nina (*shy*) It's not a threat.

She snuggles up.

Int: **Mark**'s *flat – living room to bathroom to bedroom. Night.*

Music: Bach's Keyboard Concerto No 7, Andante.

The dead of night.

The dining table has the remains of spaghetti, some wine. The bathroom has a new toothbrush.

Mark *and* **Nina** *are in bed.*

Int: **Nina***'s flat – hall to bedroom to living room to bathroom. Dawn.*

Nina *lets herself in.*

Music: Bach Sonata No 3 for cello and piano.

She hurries from room to room. **Jamie***'s not there.*

The living room is completely empty save for the piano and the cello and a vase with **Mark***'s blood red roses somehow salvaged.*

Nina Jamie. Jamie. Jamie.

Int:/Ext: **Nina***'s living room. Morning.*

Nina*, changed, showered, sits in the empty living room. She watches the clouds sail by. She closes the window.*

Int: **Nina***'s living room. Morning.*

Nina *kneels on the floor and scrubs the floorboards. A soapy bucket beside her.*

A rat appears on the mantelpiece. They regard each other.

Int: **Nina***'s hall and living room. Early evening.*

Nina *reverently puts* **Jamie***'s cello into its case.*

She dials a telephone number. **Mark***'s.*

Nina Hi. It's me. Can you come and get me?

Mark (*VO*) Oh hi. Er, no, I can't. Sorry.

Nina Oh, okay.

Mark (*VO*) Because actually I don't know where you live. Bit of a problem.

Nina It's 6A Ellingham Road.

Mark (*VO*) Where's that?

Nina N6.

Mark (*VO*) Highgate. Okay. What, shall I come now, or what?

Nina Okay.

Mark (*VO*) Right. I'm on my way. Pack your toothbrush.

The music takes over. The Andante from Bach's Keyboard Concerto No 7, a celebration.

*Ext: Outside **Nina**'s flat. Night.*

Mark's car drives up.

The music continues.

*Int: **Nina**'s living room. Night.*

Nina *looks around the room, the boards, the cello, the roses. Turns out the light. Goes out.*

The music continues.

Jamie *and the **Ghosts** file across the room towards the window.*

*Ext: Outside **Nina**'s flat. Night.*

Nina *emerges in a jacket. **Mark** has come out. She goes to him. They embrace.*

*At the window of the front room the **Ghosts** have assembled. They fill the window. **Jamie**, surrounded by **Freddie**, **Pierre**, **Isaac**, **Bruno** and co, watches as **Nina** embraces her lover. He is smiling and crying all at once. So are his friends who clap his back and support him, hand slaps of salute. It's a victory.*

Jamie's *face is awash with tears.*

The music plays.